A Guide to
Living Mortgage & Rent Free:
Through College & Beyond

By Janay Boucan

A Guide to Living Mortgage & Rent Free: Through College & Beyond

ISBN-13: 978-1-7337142-0-4

Cover photo credit: Virtuance

Dedication

I want to dedicate this book to you, the reader! I hope you are inspired and learn something new that will greatly help you in your life.

I also want to dedicate this book to the student affairs professionals, resident assistants, and college students I have interacted and worked with throughout my life. You have truly positively impacted me, and I am forever grateful.

A huge thank you to all the real estate professionals who have helped me get to this point in my career.

And most importantly, I want to thank my husband, family, and friends for loving and supporting me during all my endeavors!

Contents

Chapter 1
Student Affairs

I'm currently twenty-eight, and I've been living mortgage and rent free for the last eight years. That's right! Eight entire years! You're probably asking, "How in the world are you living mortgage/rent free?" I'm glad you asked.

It all started when I was born into student affairs—literally! If you don't know what student affairs is, let me explain. Student affairs is the absolute best department at a college/university because it has the most impact on college students outside of the classroom. The people in student affairs focus on the student holistically—mentally, emotionally, physically, and spiritually.

Since I grew up in this type of environment, it matured me, exposed me to a variety of people and cultures, and most importantly it built character and interpersonal skills.

My mother worked in student affairs as a resident assistant (RA) while I was baking in her tummy. My mother was married, a member of Alpha Kappa Alpha Sorority Incorporated, and a resident assistant at Montclair State University in Montclair, New Jersey, when she gave birth to me. As an RA, my mother mentored college students. She helped them acclimate to college through social, academic, and spontaneous programs, and even helped students when they were in crisis.

While helping students, she was compensated with free room and board, which means she was able to live for free and eat for free!

"They have jobs like that in college?" you ask? Absolutely, especially at public/state colleges and universities!

After she graduated, she applied for and became a resident director (RD) at Miami University in Miami, Ohio. This time she was responsible for supervising the resident assistants. Her compensation was her salary, living for free, eating for free, plus a 401k and health insurance.

My younger sister and I lived on campus with her, and we were stars on campus.

My mother continued up the student affairs ladder, still living and eating for free in addition to her salaried position with benefits.

I became an RA when I was a sophomore at Georgia State University. That's the typical time for the position, though the process really starts during your freshman year.

If you want to become a resident assistant, it is imperative that during your freshman year you live on campus, do well in your classes, get involved on campus, and that you attend RA learning programs. Then, when it's time to interview for the RA position, these experiences show that you are well-rounded. Also, your

RA can write a recommendation letter for you, which really helps.

But there's hope if you don't live on campus your first year. During my freshman year, I lived off campus because I didn't apply for housing in time. So my situation was not the typical process and I still got the job. Again, there's hope!

Lesson #1—Make sure you have money for a housing deposit so that you can live on campus each year.

Since I missed the deadline to pay a deposit, I had to live off campus in a student housing apartment. I had to pay $800 per month to live in a four-bedroom, four-bathroom apartment. I lived with three other students, and we all shared the common areas, the living room and kitchen. I paid rent with my refund check, which is the remaining amount of money that I received after my financial aid paid my tuition and fees, and with my part-time job.

I also applied for and received a credit card. With it I only charged my cell phone bill every month and paid it off every month. This credit card helped my credit score, because one of the factors of a credit score is the length of credit history. So by the time I graduated, my credit score was 700+.

Because of the student housing apartment experience, I saved money for the housing deposit for my sophomore year. I completed a housing application, paid the deposit, and was able to live on campus in a two-bedroom, two-bathroom apartment in the Commons, which is a residence hall at Georgia State University.

While living there, I was involved on campus as a student leader for the Outlet College Ministry, which was an organization under New Birth Missionary Baptist Church in Lithonia, Georgia, under the late Bishop Eddie L. Long. As a student leader, I helped plan several programs and became known for making brunch to encourage students to join our organization and get involved.

I continued doing this throughout the semester and also attended my RA programs without fail.

Lesson #2—Strive for A's and B's, get involved on campus, and attend your RA programs.

4

My consistent attendance at the RA programs came in handy because, in the middle of the semester, a few RA positions opened, and my RA asked me if I was interested in being an RA. I said, "Absolutely!" She told me to e-mail the resident director where there was an opening.

Immediately I e-mailed the RD my resume and scheduled an interview.

When they interviewed me for the position, they asked me questions about my involvement on campus, how I dealt with conflict, how I built relationships with others, how were my administrative skills, and so on.

Guess who got the job? Me! Why? Because of what I mentioned earlier. I had good grades, I was involved on campus, I knew how to handle conflict because of my experience with my part-time job, I knew how to build relationships as a student leader, and the like. (See "Resources" at the end of the book for a list of potential interview questions.)

Chapter 2
Being a Resident Assistant

When I became an RA, it was a challenge. Why? I was a mid-year hire, which means the RA before me either resigned or was fired, and unfortunately the RA before me was fired!

This made it hard for me because our residents loved her, so much that they felt they would betray her if they got to know me. Some of them gave me the cold shoulder and ignored me. I had a solution to that—food! I loved making breakfast. I cooked it at midnight so that no one had an excuse to miss out, like being in class or going to the gym. Sometimes I planned it and sometimes it was spontaneous. After a while they warmed up to me . . . and then they wouldn't get out of my room! Ha-ha!

As an RA, you are responsible for mentoring the residents on your floor, and sometimes you will have to deal with people in crisis. The first serious situation I had to deal with as an RA was domestic violence, and I hadn't even been there a week!

One of my residents was physically assaulted by her boyfriend, and I had to report it. This caused conflict between my resident and me because she didn't want me to tell anyone, but anytime someone is harmed or causes harm to themselves, we must report it. Period. After reporting it, the two weren't allowed to communicate with each other or see each other in person. They knew that if I saw them together in the building that I would have to report it.

Lesson #3—Don't be afraid to confront inappropriate behavior.

A couple of days later, I saw the young man on my floor with my resident, and I had to report it. Unfortunately, both residents were kicked out of housing, and my former resident was very upset with me.

You can only imagine how I felt because I'd just started this position, and it seemed like I was a snitch. But I only followed the rules to ensure a safe and comfortable environment for everyone.

To finish the story, it soon became unsafe for me, because the male friend who tried to help my resident move her things started stalking me. On my door I listed my RA phone number so my residents could call me, but he saw it and called me. After I told him I was in a relationship, he showed up the next day at the front desk, claimed that he was my boyfriend, and tried to come to my room and see me. Thank God, one of my coworkers was working at the front desk that day, could tell something was wrong, and didn't let him upstairs to my room, which would've been a violation. When I discovered that all of this had occurred, I told my supervisor, "I didn't sign up for this!" We laughed about it, but I was so serious!

After two years of being an RA for first-year students, I was ready for a change. During my senior year, I was an RA for family housing, which was for students who had families. It was amazing! We had family dinners, went to the Georgia Aquarium, and also visited the children's museum. We had a great time together. We were truly like a family and keep in touch on Facebook to this day.

During my senior year, I was really excited about applying for resident director positions, but there weren't many available when I was applying. Most required a master's degree, and most entry-level positions without a master's degree didn't pay that well.

Also during my senior year, my supervisor told me about a website, www.paycheckcity.com, which helped me calculate my salary and budget on a monthly basis. This website was very beneficial because it took out the taxes and allowed me to calculate my 401k contributions each month.

I also used www.mint.com to manage my budget, and I was able to set up financial goals like paying off credit card debt, saving money for trips, and saving for a house.

Lesson #4—It's never too early to start budgeting.

Chapter 3
College Graduate Car Programs and Living Mortgage/Rent Free After Graduation

After I graduated, I wanted to continue in student affairs, so I applied to be a resident director at Florida Southern College in Lakeland, Florida. I accepted the Greek Village Hall director position, where I would have a salary, free apartment, free food, 401k, and health insurance.

But before I moved to Florida, I applied for a car through the Nissan Graduate Program, a program for those who have graduated within the past twenty-four months or plan on graduating within six months. You also must submit proof of employment. So, at age twenty-two, I purchased my very own Nissan Altima Coupe, and my interest rate was 1.9%.

Interest rates are very important when you purchase a house, car, or have a credit card, because you could potentially pay double on the amount you borrowed. Especially with a car, because a car depreciates as soon as you drive it off the lot.

Purchasing the car was truly a simple process. I went to the dealership, showed proof that I graduated, and showed them my employment letter.

However, I hadn't expected that the monthly payment would be so much, and I hadn't expected the additional thousands of dollars and fees added to the base price of the car. So make sure you are aware of all costs before you sign the paperwork.

Other programs, like the Toyota and Honda Graduate Program, had 0% interest rates.

After I purchased my car, I packed up all my belongings and drove to Lakeland, Florida.

When I first started at Florida Southern College, I thought it was going to be challenging because I wasn't Greek. But from my training and experience I knew the goal would be to build relationships with students no matter our backgrounds, and to create an intentional and respectful environment.

One of my favorite programs, which I adopted from my former supervisors, was the Community Cash Silent Auction. Throughout the year, my staff and I gave out Community Cash to students who were studious, attended programs, helped their RAs with bulletin boards, and students who were helpful by picking up trash, planning their own programs, being leaders, and the like. At the end of the school year, my staff and I went to Ross and bought prizes that the students would appreciate, and then we set out those items at the Silent Auction. There the students used their Community Cash to bid on different prizes. If they had the highest bid, they won the prize.

This program really encouraged students to get involved, and they were rewarded for it.

Lesson #5—The goal is to build relationships and create a family environment.

After a year working as a resident director, I wanted to pursue social work. I applied for the Master of Social Work (MSW) Program at the University of Georgia, and I also applied for the graduate assistantship position, specifically graduate resident, through UGA's Housing Department. I was accepted to both.

Chapter 4
$100 Master's Degree

I paid $100 for my master's degree. How? Two words: graduate assistantships. Graduate assistantships are employment opportunities in different departments for graduate students. In exchange for graduate students working a certain number of hours per week for the department, they are compensated with a tuition waiver and a monthly stipend.

The best graduate assistantships are the housing graduate assistantships! Why? Because you get free room and board, a monthly stipend, and a tuition waiver. But, this time you must supervise RAs. No problem! I loved my job and truly enjoyed supervising my seven RAs and being a mentor to twenty other RAs.

I also took a study-abroad trip to Ghana for three weeks, and my tuition was $25. Of course, I had to pay for the flight and the other fees, but my tuition was only $25, so technically I paid $125 for my master's degree, but who's counting?

As a graduate resident at UGA, I had the pleasure of working in a first-year high-rise called Creswell Hall. I worked with more than twenty-five RAs, three other graduate residents, a hall director, an area coordinator, and more than nine hundred first-year students.

We dealt with everything you can think of. One night I swatted wasps with a tennis racket because they built their nests on top of the building and came through the window seals. I also had to deal with the aftermath of "Saturdays in Athens," which are the UGA game days, and those were very eventful. Go Dawgs!

Chapter 5
$18,000 House

After I graduated from UGA, I applied for the resident director position at Spelman College, the number-one historically black college/university (HBCU) for women. I was offered the position and I accepted. As resident director I oversaw Howard-Harreld Hall, the largest first-year hall on campus.

It was the most amazing experience ever! I supervised seven resident assistants, and I was responsible for more than 180 first-year residents. We were the most active and the best hall at Spelman College. "HH! PHI BETA!" was our chant! We implemented Motivational Mondays, where we put encouraging notes on bathroom mirrors every Monday to uplift our residents.

We also implemented Pancakes & Post Secrets, where my staff and I made pancakes and our residents anonymously posted secrets that they've never told anyone, such as, "I've never had a boyfriend/girlfriend before," and "I'm homesick," or more serious situations like, "I was in an abusive relationship."

After we posted the notes, we asked others who could relate to put a sticker on the note to let people know that they are not alone.

We also posted on-campus resources like counseling so that students could speak to a professional if they needed help. I had an amazing staff, and we still keep in contact to this day.

As a resident director, I was compensated with a salary, a free apartment, free food, 401k, health insurance, and a free work phone. My husband also moved in with me and I was able to have an emotional support animal, a "morkie" (yorkshire terrier and maltese mix), named Ava. Ava brought so much joy to the students at Spelman College and the ladies at City of Refuge.

This compensation gave me the ability and flexibility to save money for traveling. I was able to go to the Bahamas, Jamaica, Mexico, Dominican Republic, New Orleans, and I happily used Groupon for all my trips because it included the flight, all food, and nights at the resorts.

In partnership with four other trusted people, I was also able to invest in properties. I purchased my first rental property for $18,000! Yes, you read that right, $18,000! My car had cost more than my first rental property! We bought a two-bedroom, one-bathroom bungalow with a front porch and a large backyard for $18,000, though it had been listed for $30,000. It only cost us $7,000 to make it move-in ready.

Lesson #6—Save your college refund checks for investment opportunities.

We were able to negotiate the price because the house needed a new roof and there was mold in the crawlspace. We made minor repairs, fully furnished the property, and then marketed it to college students. We charged an all-inclusive price of $700 per room, and that included all utilities, washer/dryer, cable, Wi-Fi, and an alarm system.

ATLANTA BELTLINE COMMUNITY
STUDENT HOUSING

Lesson #7—Don't be afraid to negotiate and ask for what you want.

We were so excited about that property that we purchased three more investment properties—in three months. We purchased our second property for $26,154 in

February, our third property for $25,000 in March, and our fourth property for $21,500 in April.

How did we do this? Peer money lenders and credit cards. My credit score was 787, and I was able to get approved for these loans because of my credit history and my career.

We renovated the other three properties for about $20,000 each and started marketing to college students during the summer. However, after some discussion and challenges with the third property, we decided to "buy and hold" the third property.

At Spelman, resident directors don't have to work during the summers and were still paid a salary, so I started working for City of Refuge (COR), helping human and sex trafficking survivors. This was an amazing experience because I was able to really use my social work degree by helping underserved populations.

At this point I was renovating properties during the day and working at COR in the evening, and still getting paid from Spelman College.

Chapter 6
More Benefits and Insights

After having some challenges with the third property, we attempted to sell it for a profit. However, it ended up being a loss. We purchased it for $25,000, completed about $20,000 worth of renovations, and sold it for $42,500. So it was a $2,500 loss, but I was able to pay for my $10,000 destination wedding in Cancun, Mexico—everything included. This included my dress, the wedding ceremony, the reception, flight, all food, and the nights at the resort. We had about fifty guests, including our bridal party, and the trip was affordable for them as well.

If you make the decision to be a resident assistant, it will be the most rewarding job you will ever have! This position allows you to meet so many people from around the nation and world, and you get to make a positive impact on people's lives. You are there for students at their best and their worst. If you love people, enjoy creating a family environment, and have patience, you will do great in this position.

Through the RA position, you'll also build many transferable skills—talents and abilities you can use when you transition to another job or career.

I want to be clear: Being an RA is not easy. Why? Because as an RA your goal is to help others, and sometimes you have to handle complicated problems. So it's important to take care of yourself and take time for yourself. It's also important to be a team player, because the other RAs will be your family!

RAs deal with students who are struggling with classes, homesickness, roommate conflicts, cleanliness, parties, illegal substances, domestic violence, sexual assault, mental health, suicidal ideation, and more!

There will also be nights when you'll be on duty and responsible for interacting with residents in your building, submitting maintenance requests, and handling and reporting incidents.

I know this sounds like a lot, but you will get trained on all of this! I always told my staff, if you can be an RA, you can be anything!

Could this be the destination for you in college?

If you make the decision to become a resident director, it's imperative that you are approachable, relatable, and solution-oriented. A resident director works 24/7, and most of your day will be spent supervising your staff, interacting with students, and resolving conflict. You will also have administrative work, such as incident reporting, checking in/out students, and you'll be responsible for leadership councils. Depending on the policies, you may have to go to the hospital with a student, interact with parents, and more.

You will also have to adjust to working and living in the same place, which is not an easy task. If you have your immediate family living with you, that may be an adjustment as well. You must learn how to separate work and home.

You must also create boundaries. Creating boundaries with your staff and residents is very important because you can get burned out fast and it may appear that you're showing favoritism. You must be consistent in everything you do.

It's also important that you set expectations right at the beginning. When I was an RD, my staff knew my expectations, particularly that we would not be mediocre. I believed in intentional and passive programming and focusing on each student's needs. I was focused on building relationships more than anything else, because that's what student affairs is all about.

Resources

Several pages of valuable resources follow to answer some of the questions you may have.

Below, I have provided some questions that you may be asked during an interview to become a resident assistant, followed by questions that may be asked during an interview to become a resident director. Every college/university has a different process for interviewing. However, these are common questions asked of prospective RAs and RDs.

Practice: Possible Resident Assistant Interview Questions

1. Tell us about yourself.
2. Why are you interested in the resident assistant position?
3. Are you involved on campus? If so, do you think your activities will interfere with the RA position?
4. What are your strengths and weaknesses?
5. How do you manage your time?
6. How do you relieve stress?
7. How do you handle conflict? How would you handle conflict with a coworker or a supervisor? Give an example.

8. Tell us about a time you worked in a group and explain your role.
9. What does inclusivity mean to you? What does diversity mean to you?
10. How would you build relationships with your residents? How would you help your residents build relationships with each other?
11. Describe your ability to pay attention, follow through, and meet deadlines.
12. If you had to plan a social/academic program for first-year students, what would you do? What would you do for upperclassmen?
13. What was your favorite program that your RA planned or your favorite on-campus program?

Practice: Possible Resident Director Interview Questions

1. Tell us about yourself.
2. Why are you interested in the resident director position?
3. What is your management/supervisory style?
4. If you had a list of things to do that had to be completed by the end of the day, how would you make sure it all got done?
5. What are your strengths and weaknesses?
6. Give an example of a goal you reached and tell me how you achieved it.
7. Give an example of a goal you didn't meet and how you handled it.
8. How do you handle stress? Give an example of a stressful situation and how you handled it.
9. Describe a decision you made that was unpopular and how you handled implementing it.
10. Have you ever dealt with company policy you weren't in agreement with? How did you handle it?
11. What do you do when your schedule is interrupted? Give an example of how you handle it.
12. Have you had to convince a team to work on a project they weren't thrilled about? How did you do it?

13. Give an example of how you've worked on a team.
14. Have you handled a difficult situation with a coworker? How?

Most colleges/universities are moving toward behavioral interview questions, which means they want to see your thought process for handling a situation. According to the Balance Careers website, research says use the "STAR" technique:

1. **(S) Situation.** Describe the situation in which the event took place.
2. **(T) Task.** Describe the task you were asked to complete.
3. **(A) Action.** Explain what action you took to complete the task or solve the problem.
4. **(R) Results.** Explain the result of your actions.[1]

---

[1] Source: Sarah Cook, *Coaching for High Performance: How to Develop Exceptional Results Through Coaching* (IT Governance Publishing, 2009).

Salary Job? How to Estimate Your
Hourly Take-home Pay

When you apply for salary-based careers, you can do the following to estimate your hourly pay.

- Go to www.paycheckcity.com and click "Salary Calculator"
  - Under "State for withholding" pick your state
  - Under "Gross Pay" enter how much you make
  - Pick your "Pay Frequency"
  - Change anything else that may apply
- Add "Deductions" (if they apply)
  - If you have a 401k, health insurance, or any other deductions, enter the name and the amount by fixed or percentage
- Calculate
  - Click "Calculate" and it will give you a pretty accurate amount of money that you will make per hour after taxes, deductions, and the like, based on a forty-hour work week

Hourly Job? How to Estimate Your Yearly Take-home Pay

If you are applying for hourly-based careers, you can do the following to estimate your yearly take-home pay.

- Go to www.paycheckcity.com and click "Hourly Calculator"
  - Under "State for withholding" pick your state
  - Enter your "Pay Rate"
  - Enter how many hours you work or "160" hours for the month
  - Change anything else that may apply
- Add "Deductions" (if they apply)
  - If you have a 401k, health insurance, or any other deductions, enter the name and the amount by fixed or percentage
- Calculate
  - Click "Calculate" and it will give you a pretty accurate amount of money that you make after taxes, deductions, and the like

Need an Easy Way to Manage Finances and Bills?
Try Mint

- Create a free and safe account with www.mint.com and download the Mint app
- Enter all of your accounts
  - bank accounts
  - 401k/investments
  - expenses/bills (car payment/insurance, cable, and so on)
  - student loans
- Click "Trends" and you will see your spending habits
  - Disclaimer: Mint.com will heighten your awareness because it will demonstrate your spending habits and force you to reflect on your wants, needs, and living within your means. However, it is a great accountability partner.
- Next, click on "Budget," enter your income, and then start entering all your expenses
- Start creating goals like paying off debt, saving for a house/car, taking a trip, saving for a wedding, emergency savings, or whatever you need
- Financial S.M.A.R.T goals are SO important and it's important you stay on track!!!

- o Create a "Custom Goal" for your wedding, furniture, electronics, babies/kids, gifts/shopping, and so on
- Money-saving financial tips:
  - o Do you live in Atlanta and want to buy a home instead of rent? Hire a licensed realtor.
  - o Want to buy a car and you're a recent college graduate? Check out Honda, Toyota, and Nissan Graduate Programs.
  - o Want to take a trip? Use Groupon or Travel Zoo.
  - o If you're trying to pay off credit cards, try to pay off the card with the highest interest rate first.
  - o Pay more than the minimum on your credit card, or it will take forever to pay off the loan because the interest is accruing
  - o If you're saving for retirement, choose the percentage that your employer will match because that's free money
  - o Save for an emergency, which means you should have three to six months' worth of expenses saved. For example, if your monthly expenses are $1,000, you should have $3k-$6k in your savings account.
- Paying off debt:

- o Mint does an amazing job of calculating the interest that you will pay overtime and how much you save over time
- o Here's an example of a $13,900 credit card with a 17.99% interest rate
  - · If you pay the minimum of $500, it will take three years and you will end up paying $4,141 in interest
  - · If you pay $1K/month, it will take one year and three months, and you will save $2,392 in interest
  - · Mint will provide a visual graph so you can see the difference in paying the minimum or more, and It wlll show you the interest that you will save
- If this is a challenge for you, you have options— call your bank and ask for a lower interest rate and/or apply for a balance transfer through another bank

Valuable Insights: Checking and Savings Accounts

- Find a credit union/bank with no monthly maintenance fees for your checking/savings account
- I use Capital One 360 Savings Accounts because they force me to save. If I want to get money out of my account, I must go to a CVS, Walgreens, Kroger, or Rite Aid. It also takes a couple of days before the money is available for use.
- Capital One 360 Savings Accounts offer a 0.75% interest rate on your savings, compared to Bank of America that has a 0.01% interest rate.
- Any credit cards or loans with high interest rates are the *devil*!
- Always pay more than the minimum payment
- Call your bank and ask for a lower interest rate
- Every six months, you can apply for a credit line increase, which will be a soft inquiry on your credit report, but it will increase your credit card utilization, which increases your credit score. **This doesn't mean that you need to keep spending money; your credit utilization should be under 30%!**

Valuable Insights: Credit Score

- Keep your credit card utilization under 30%
- Pay all your bills on time (at least a few days before their due date). If you're going to be late, then you need to call and ask to make payment arrangements.
- Don't let your medical bills go to collections; apply for financial assistance
- Dispute all the inaccurate remarks on your credit report through the big three credit bureaus, and also Credit Karma

Dispute Letter Example

Experian
P.O Box 9701
Allen, TX 75013

To Whom It May Concern:

I have thoroughly reviewed my credit report, and I would like to inform you of the inaccuracies it contains (see list below). I am requesting, under the provisions of the Fair Credit Reporting Act (FCRA), 15 USC section 1681i, that you investigate these accounts.

Accounts:

- Bank of America, account number 1234567890
- Nissan Finance, account number 1234567890
- Chase Bank, account number 1234567890

Reason: This collection is inaccurate.

I understand that failure to investigate these accounts within a period of thirty days will result in "non-verification," which requires that the above accounts be immediately removed from my credit file. I also understand that the Fair Credit Reporting Act, specifically 15 USC SECTIONS 1681i(d) updates credit reports at no charge.

Thank you for your time and attention to this matter. I look forward to hearing from you soon.

The Basics of Real Estate Investment

- For my four rental properties:
  - ○ I received financing through Lending Club, Circleback Lending (no longer exists), and my credit cards to purchase the properties
  - ○ My credit score was a 773 when I applied for all financing
  - ○ Checking your rate for Lending Club and other peer lenders doesn't affect your credit score, unless you accept the loan
  - ○ If you accept the loan, it will be on your credit report and the interest rate will be high, so make sure you can afford that monthly payment
- Want to "fix and flip" a home?
  - ○ Hire a licensed real estate agent that is efficient
  - ○ Find a trusted friend, family member, business partner
  - ○ Apply for a personal loan through your bank and/or other financing companies
  - ○ Look for houses, have cash ready, put in an offer, and have at least five *licensed*, quality contractors give you quotes for repairs and updates

- Purchase the home, obtain permits through the county, renovate, stage, and sell it based on the comparable properties in the area

About the Author

Janay Boucan is a real estate investor, property manager, and a real estate agent who has been investing in real estate since 2015. She is the proud owner of SJB Investments, LLC, a company that purchases and renovates abandoned properties in the metro Atlanta area. Ms. Boucan buys properties near t Atlanta Beltline, the Mercedes-Benz Stadium, and local colleges and universities and then sells these properties to families and/or leases them by room to college students.

She can help you with all of your real estate needs—whether you are a first-time home buyer or a first-time investor!

She has served in student affairs, specifically the Housing and Residence Life Department, since January 2010. For the past six years, Ms. Boucan served as a resident director and she managed residence halls, supervised resident assistants, reported maintenance issues, and helped students in crisis. Janay also enjoyed the benefits of free room and board in addition to a salary, but now she wants to bridge the gap by providing affordable housing to those in need.

Ms. Boucan has exceptional interpersonal and conflict-management skills, and she enjoys creating and building relationships with her ladies at Spelman

College and ladies at City of Refuge through credit repair, budgeting, and real estate investments. Janay says, "It would be my pleasure to serve you!"

Janay Boucan is also in the Master of Science in Commercial Real Estate (MSCRE) Program, specializing in property management and project management at Georgia State University and will be graduating in August 2019.

www.ingramcontent.com/pod-product-compliance
Lightning Source LLC
LaVergne TN
LVHW051204080426
835508LV00021B/2807